Sounds
of
Fury

Compiled by Donald Hilton

Sounds of Fury

an anthology of material
by young people of the
Fellowship of United Reformed Youth
and their friends

compiled by Donald Hilton

Other anthologies compiled by Donald Hilton
Liturgy of Life
Flowing Streams
Prayers for the Church Community
(with Roy Chapman)
published by the National Christian Education Council

ISBN 0 85346 136 8

Published by the United Reformed church,
86 Tavistock Place, London WC1H 9RT

Printed by Witney Press Ltd
Cover and illustrations by Sara Broughton

Contents

Preface

In the period when I was Youth and Children's Secretary for the Congregational Church it became clear to me that many people - younger and older - have latent gifts of writing which not all find the opportunity to express.

In the intervening years that conviction has increased and one result has been a series of anthologies, published by the National Christian Education Council, each of which contains material from both recognised and new authors.

SOUNDS OF FURY is a further example. Members of our church were challenged to write poetry or prose around the five words that underlie much of the thinking of FURY; Learning, Worship, Prayer, Giving and Involvement.

However, this is not a book written by young people. It would be alien to the youth policy of the United Reformed Church to have made it so. We do not see young people in isolation; we see them in community. The work of older and younger people mingle in this volume just as we expect to see the insights of younger and older mingle in local churches, District Councils, Synods and the General Assembly.

The primary aim of the anthology? To provide material for private and public worship and study groups wherever United Reformed Church people meet.

Donald Hilton

Foreword

The United Reformed Church is celebrating youthfulness and its own young people, the Fellowship of United Reformed Youth.

In the 1990s, the church has built a National Youth Resource Centre at Yardley Hastings in Northamptonshire. This is being used as a base for exciting challenges to young people and to their older friends, as they go together along the great Christian pilgrimage. A bright and cheerful pack called *The Hitch-Hiker's Guide to the Gospel* is providing material to help young people along the way in their local church and community. The FURY Council is a new representative body where young people make decisions and carry them out. They run FURY themselves and work with young people in other churches and secular groups. So there is good cause for celebration!

Sounds of FURY is part of that celebration. Contributions have come in from people in many places. Not all the writers are young, but all have written of matters relevant to young people now.

We are delighted that Donald Hilton, in his year as Moderator of General Assembly, has been able to complete this volume. Donald has used his renowned gift of words and his skills in ordering material so that it can be readily accessible for use. He shows how the policy of our church in *The Basis for Union* is being carried out in the work of its own young people.

The sections are based on the five words that underlie the work and thinking of FURY: Worship, Prayer, Learning, Giving and Involvement. This format makes the material user-friendly in worship and for personal spiritual growth and prayer.

May all the readers find their own reasons here to celebrate!

Ruth Clarke
Convener, Youth Committee

Solomon answered, "You always showed great love for my father David, your servant, and he was good, loyal, and honest in his relations with you. And you have continued to show him your great and constant love by giving him a son who today rules in his place.

0 Lord God, you have let me succeed my father as king, even though I am very young and don't know how to rule.

Here I am among the people you have chosen to be your own, a people who are so many that they cannot be counted.

So give me the wisdom I need to rule your people with justice and to know the difference between good and evil. Otherwise, how would I ever be able to rule this great people of yours?"

1 Kings 3. 6-9

Happy are those who know they are spiritually poor;
the Kingdom of heaven belongs to them!

Happy are those who mourn:
God will comfort them!

Happy are those who are humble;
they will receive what God has promised!

Happy are those whose greatest desire is to do what God requires;
God will satisfy them fully!

Happy are those who are merciful to others;
God will be merciful to them!

Happy are the pure in heart;
they will see God!

Happy are those who work for peace;
God will call them his children!

Happy are those who are persecuted because they do what God requires;
the Kingdom of heaven belongs to them!

Happy are you when people insult you and persecute you and tell all kinds of evil lies against you because you are my followers.

Matthew 5. 3-11

The United Reformed Church, under the authority of Holy Scripture and in corporate responsibility to Jesus Christ its everliving head, acknowledges its duty to be open at all times to the leading of the Holy Spirit and therefore affirms its right to make such new declaration of its faith and for such purposes as may from time to time be required by obedience to the same Spirit.

At the same time the United Reformed Church accepts with thanksgiving the witness borne to the catholic faith by the Apostles' and Nicene Creeds. It recognises as its own particular heritage the formulations and declarations of faith which have been valued by Congregationalists, Presbyterians and members of Churches of Christ as stating the Gospel and seeking to make its implications clear.

URC Manual, p.6; para.18.

1

A child of three beginning to learn
What God is all about
What does He look like, where is He?
You get asked from time to time.

A four year old beginning to draw,
This is a picture of God, he says,
There on the paper a head and a body
As this child is seeing Him.

A five year old who is writing
describes Him in lots of way.
He's a person who's up in the sky
Who we talk to in prayer.

A fifteen year old worried with life,
Upset over the break-up with a girlfriend
not sure quite what to do
about keeping his image with friends,
Asking God what life is about.

A forty year old upset with God,
How could He let the world go on
With famine, war and death?.
Why doesn't He help?

At eighty, at peace with God,
talking to Him in silent prayer,
feeling the tranquillity of His being there,
Close at their side.

Wendy Manners

2   Never too early, never too late.

It's never too early, it's never too late
To go on a journey to grow in the faith:
To see what the God of surprises can do
The glorious future that's waiting for you.
It's never too late to start over again;
Enjoy the adventure of challenge and change;
To climb to the heights and to take in the view -
It's never too early, it's never too late for you.

Life is a journey; a chance to explore
The treasure within us and what lies in store;
Outside the door -
Such wonderful horizons to be seen;
Beyond our wildest dreams
Of what the kingdom means.

With every moment, at every turn
The wilderness blossoms with lessons to learn
And bushes burn -
For God is there if we have eyes to see
Showing you and me
The people we could be

Jesus the way, the truth, and the vine
Offers life in its fulness, and gives us a sign;
The water's wine! -
So life for us may never be the same
If we dare to change
To step out in His name.

Martin John Nicholls

3   I'm not talented!

I'm not talented,
In any way at all.
My mum says when I was 5
I could only just crawl.

I'm not talented,
In any way whatsoever,
My teacher says I'm no good at sport,
And I am certainly not clever.

I'm not talented,
There's no doubt about it,
I went to school to collect my pen,
And then went home without it.

I'm not talented,
Grade E is what I'm rated.
I took the teacher a note from my mum,
Which the headmaster confiscated.

I'm not talented,
In any way at all,
But I've got three jobs and a law degree,
Now that I've left school.

Anna Oldershaw

4   As a Child   **Mark 10. 15**

I must change
Into a child
To enter your Kingdom.

Always being told
What to do
What not to do.

Bullied by others
Pushed around
Called names.

Unable to communicate
Cannot think logically
Talking nonsense.

Tears replacing laughter
Falling on my knees
Falling out with friends.

Frustrated by others
Confused by rules
Too young to understand.

Must I change
Into a child
To enter your Kingdom?

Melanie Smith

5 Discovery

She ambled into the room and saw his minute frame perched on
the end of a stool.
His wide, icy blue eyes rose to greet hers,
And with a painted smile, false, like a china doll,
She cocooned her hands around his face,
Her palms gently stroking away the stains from his tears.
Was it any reassurance?

Her motionless body allowed her to twirl the golden locks,
Normally bouncing on his head, today lifeless and flat.
Every part of his small world shattered,
Every part of him drained.

It was no easier for her though,
Her mind was flickering, incapable of concentrating,
Losing its grasp on reality.
She was the one who had to confront her five year old son
with the unmistakable truth that his father was dead.

She knew resenting herself was ridiculous,
But it was she who had forced him to face the idea of death.
Knowing that this discovery would take away a little innocence,
a little of his youth.
And gently refocusing her gaze on him, she saw the determined
far away look in his eyes.
And could almost feel the momentum of his imagination,
Exploring the endless possibilities of death.
How useless she felt, how pathetic.

Then like a small bird just finding its voice, he quietly chirped
"I think Daddy still loves us wherever he is"
Her eyes gabled on her forehead, perhaps mostly from surprise.
This was something so simple, something she'd been unable
to recognise.
Instantly she dropped the false smile and pretence and felt
the freedom of being herself.
Able to share her grief.

He wriggled closer and enveloped himself in her arms,
Seeking the security of her touch.
As for her, she was content to sit holding him.
Because this way, she, too, was able to find the safety
in his small warm hold.

Rebekah Slow

6 "I'm afraid your Nan died in her sleep last night". The words echo round my head but don't really reach my heart. It's alright, I can cope, I've got to be strong. I knew it was coming. I'm prepared for this. I've been waiting for the call.

But it still hurts.

It's final now, there's no last chance, no hope to hold on to. That's it. No soft smile from the hospital bed; no hand to hold to comfort; no more torture though the Endless Pain has found it's End.

Then the sadness. I know it was for the best, but I still want her back. It may be selfish because she is now at peace but I want her back.

The words of comfort flow. The care and love of fellow Christians overwhelms. "Yes I'm alright" I say, "It was for the best". The words tumble from my lips like a prepared speech, but do I really feel them?

How can I enjoy life now? If I am happy I feel I should be sad. Then it's time to say a final goodbye. It's too sad, much too sad. But I'm alright. I can cope. I have to cope for my Dad's sake. He must feel worse than I do.

We walk behind the coffin; she is in there, she is really in there. Not still in the hospital bed awaiting my visit. She is in there.

The faces turn, concern and care written across them and that's when the coping is over. I can't cope. I'm not alright. I'm sad and I want to let it all go.

Every tear takes with it an hour of pain until all the pain is washed away in a river of release.

The curtains close slowly, blocking my view of the coffin. I want to shout and scream and stop them from closing because the nearer they get to joining the further from me my Nan is. They get closer until bang, they meet and the pain explodes from my mouth in a cry of grief.

For I am certain that nothing in all creation can separate us from the love of God. Neither death nor life ....

These words cut into my thoughts and bring such comfort that I have to stop and think. At this moment I am so sad, so angry, I feel such pain but above all this comes the realisation that there is freedom from all this if I give it all to God. And when I do this His spirit lifts me, I am filled with peace and above all, the hurt is lessened.

I know that God is telling me that she is with him, that it is all for the best.

I know also that I no longer have to "Just Cope" because God is there for me in everything to give me the strength and hope I need.

Death can bring Life in all its fullness.

One Loss was also such a large Gain.

Dawn Willis

7

I am a tyre.
I am filled with spiritual air.
I am rolling along a long road.
The Devil has given me a slow puncture.
I have to be continually pumped up
By means of daily Bible reading,
Worship, fellowship and prayer.
If I am not always being pumped up
Then I deflate and slow down.
If I am left for too long,
Then I roll towards the ditches
at the sides of the road.
But I continue to be filled and so
roll along the road that leads to
eternal life with Christ.

Stephen Buttle

8　Holy Spirit
　　be with us today.
　　Let the seeds of your truth
　　break from the husks of our words.

　　Meet every individual in worship
　　and fuse us into one body.
　　With stronger trust
　　may we become more mature,
　　irritating others less
　　and serving you in new ways.

　　Enable each one of us to develop
　　the particular gift that is ours
　　so that together and separately,
　　we may all gladly confess
　　that Jesus is Lord
　　now and always.

Tony Burnham

9 God answered
     I am that I am

     Wait -
     Wait on me
     Commune -
     Commune with me
     Receive -
     Receive from me
     Trust -
     Trust in me
     Be not afraid
     For the very hairs on your head are numbered.
     You are special
     Very special to me.
     I have chosen you.

     Move on -
     Move on with me
     I will heal you
     Your love for yourself and others will be tender
     Attentive
     Colourful
     Life will be rich in all its fullness
     You will fulfill my purposes
     My promise is for you
     Dwell in me as I dwell in you.

     Deborah M Mcvey

10   Emmanuel

Anxiety:
Back in the utter darkness of the locked cellar,
Eyes tightly closed against the lurking spiders,
Unseen horrors, nameless terrors.
Alone again, my child-self frozen with fear
Unable to move,
Unable to scream,
Unable to breathe.

> *Stay with it. ....experience it. ....perhaps my*
> *good-mother-self will come to open the door,*
> *to lead me out. Or shall I? Dare I?*

And then I see You with me - why,
You don't look at all like I thought:
So ordinary, So *human*....
Slight, dark-skinned, strong features, dark eyes,
Leaning towards me, you wrap me round protectively....

"Will you lead me out?"
"Look", you say;
We have not moved - but now,
Looking away from You I see
The walls are gone:
And all is light:
Warm, glowing light, spreading like billowing clouds -
"trailing clouds of glory. .."

Recalled to the present by a drawn-out sigh
Thanksgiving and understanding combine:
You don't change our circumstances -
You stand with us in them.

June Plaice

11   Emmaus   (Luke 24: 13-35)

Every road leads to somewhere, this one to realisation and recognition,
Many journeys are just routine,
Maybe the familiar road will open up new vistas
As the two homeward went, sharing their gloom in the gathering dusk
Until joined by one who shared words and time.
Stranger He appeared to be, yet the truth would soon be out.

Eventually the journey must end and ways divide,
Must He go? - come and share a meal.
Made He the gesture of thanksgiving, breaking the bread as an offering,
At once all became clear.
Up to now they were grieving and confused,
Saviour, not stranger, was this guest, the Risen Lord.

Eagerly with new found energy and purpose they must return.
Momentous is the "Good News",
Mankind must know,
A new signpost has been raised on Calvary, pointing the way to Life,
Unless we change direction or repave the old way we are lost,
Speed us on life's journey, refreshed and redeemed.

Y Mochyn Daear

12   I was a stranger

A new place, a new time and space,
New thoughts and feelings at such a pace
What am I to make of this?
In such beauty and earthly bliss.

As a stranger I feel apart
But other wishes lie in my heart
I watch and wait and feel at ease
And know my God is here to please.

At one with this land
In rain, woods and sand
A stranger no more, of that I'm sure.

Wallie Warmington

13   Judas Iscariot

Jesus called me too to be one of the twelve,
Unlike the others I did not come from Galilee,
Did He know even then what I would do?
Always when men speak my name they think only of betrayal,
Silver I received, yet great was the price I paid,
       But not as great as what it cost Him.

       I tried to force His hand,
I thought I knew better than even God,
Satan, they said it was, who took possession of me,
Care had I of the communal purse,
Accused of stealing from my friends,
Repay what I took with blood money, that is what was said!
Indeed, I never misspent a penny, all I wanted was for Him
       to act in the way I wanted Him to do
Only He had to carry out His Father's wishes!
Terror and tragedy were my reward - for Jesus it was
       Triumph through suffering.

Y Mochyn Daear

14   Trying

I made a picture in my head
To show me what life ought to be,
What it should give me.
But it didn't.

I made a picture by the proper rules
Taught me by society
By family and school and church,
Then took a rest
And waited for it all to happen.
But it didn't.

I think I am a lousy painter
Or a lazy one.
Is it too late to try again?

W S Beattie

15 When is the end to this meaning?
Does it start at the break of the day?
Does it carry on till noon?
Does it continue to the end of the day?

No, it continues on forever
As we grow to love God even more,
And we learn to grow in understanding
About the loving arms we adore.

Elizabeth Watkins-Smith

16 Is a prison a place without windows,
A cell, a lock on a door?
Is a dungeon four closed walls around you?
A chamber the torturous score.

A prison is life without hope,
A cell is the fear to explore,
A dungeon is lack of adventure,
And a chamber is hell evermore..

Elizabeth Watkins-Smith

17 Thank you Lord for the times
when I have been lonely
and have longed for human company-
It was at these times
that I found your Holy Spirit,
always ready to offer friendship and fellowship.

Natasha Winter

18   Motor-bike Merry-go-round

Long ago... so long ago.... but clear and sharp as today
Riding the familiar, well -loved bikes,
Picking up speed. .. when suddenly
      Gut-wrenching fear!
It's going too fast...! I can't stop it...!
It's throwing me off the side, I'm slipping,
      Terror, panic - God!
Somehow, a slide-in thought flowers into action -
      "Make it go faster. .. Want it to".
A supreme, conscious effort of will - then,
Gripping, leaning forward into the ride, and
      Exultation! Exhilaration!
      "Faster, go faster!"
Wind-whipped hair, the thrill of speed, Super!
The little twelve year old learned her lesson well.

But now...
Raucous klaxon warning
Shuddering through guts and bones
Gives notice the ride is ending:
      Already the brakes are applied,
      Already the movement is slowing,
      Already the riders prepare to dismount.
This lesson is so much harder to learn:
      I must *want* the music to fade;
      I must *will* the bikes to be still;
I must let go and be ready to leave
      At the appointed time.
It's hard to say Goodbye, despite the ups and downs;
Can I alight with dignity?
      Are there any other rides?
Or shall I disappear into night's final blackness?
You have kept me company till now:
You have said You will not leave me;
      Take my hand - I'll go with You.

June Plaice

19

Father, we do not find it easy
to retain our enthusiasm
for growing and learning
for searching and discovering.
      Rekindle our desire to seek your truth.

Father, we do not find it easy
to listen to the wisdom of the world
in other cultures and traditions
in words of playwright and poet
in children's dreams
and old folks memories.
      Open our minds to receive your truth.

Thank you, Father,
for the timeless words
of the Gospel writers
with their differing perspectives
on Jesus' teaching.
      Sharpen our insight as we address today's world.

To all entrusted with teaching
our prayers reach out
that they may engage fearlessly in the search for wisdom,
that they may have skill in communication
and a genuine love for the minds and lives
of all whom they teach.

As seeds of hopes are sown,
in schools, churches, and places of further education,
by the people who glimpse your kingdom,
may people of all nations
see what no eye sees
and hear what no ear hears:
things at present beyond their mental horizon,
but in range of your loving purpose.

David Jenkins

20 A grain of wheat

In the beginning the seed
emptying the desire
to remain entirely itself
creates the new possibility of growth.

From sleep the blind roots stir,
grope outwards into the blackness;
yet part of it senses somewhere
the seemingly irrational light.

Gradually oh so slowly
it gains an upward sense of direction,
lifts a tender shoot
against the negation of gravity.

Around it grow tangled grasses and moss
taunting and trying to choke,
but this gentle growing thing
continues unheeding;
refusing to be stifled by weeds
it begins to unfold its potential -
stretching into the light
its leaves unfold to receive
the life-giving elements.

As it continues on its way
it begins to realise
that its destiny is reality;
soul-like it lifts itself
above the dark earth
that was its only dwelling place
as it travels sunwards.

Cecily Taylor

Worship

Praise the Lord!
Give thanks to the Lord, because he is good;
his love is eternal.
Who can tell all the great things he has done?
Who can praise him enough?
Happy are those who obey his commands,
who always do what is right.
Remember me, Lord, when you help your people;
include me when you save them.
Let me see the prosperity of your people
and share in the happiness of your nation,
in the glad pride of those who belong to you.

Psalm 106.1-5

How great are God's riches! How deep are his wisdom and knowledge!
Who can explain his decisions? Who can understand his ways? As the
scripture says,

> "Who knows the mind of the Lord?
> Who is able to give him advice?
> Who has ever given him anything,
> so that he had to pay it back?"

For all things were created by him, and all things exist through him and for him.
To God be the glory for ever! Amen

Romans 11.33-36

"Lord God Almighty, how great and wonderful are your deeds!
King of the nations, how right and true are your ways!
Who will not stand in fear of you, Lord?
Who will refuse to declare your greatness?
You alone are holy.
All the nations will come and worship you
because your just actions are seen by all."

Revelation 15.3-4

Within the one, holy, catholic, apostolic Church the United Reformed Church acknowledges its responsibility under God:

-     to make its life a continual offering of itself and the world to God in adoration and worship through Jesus Christ;
-     to receive and express the renewing life of the Holy Spirit in each place and in its total fellowship, and there to declare the reconciling and saving power of the life, death and resurrection of Jesus Christ.

URC Manual p.4; para.11

We believe in the one living and true God, creator, preserver and ruler of all things in heaven and earth, Father, Son and Holy Spirit. Him alone we worship, and in him we put our trust.

URC Manual p.6; para.17

The worship of the local church is an expression of the worship of the whole people of God.

URC Manual p.8; para.24

21   I worship you

It is quiet, Lord, yet I worship,
in peace there is a silent joy,
My mind and soul rise up to you
Humbled in your presence.

Someone is talking, Lord, and I worship.
Rejoicing in the presence of others,
yet alone in my address to you
As you consume all my attention.

It is noisy, Lord, I will worship.
Above the commotion I am aware of you.
There are friends, and companions, and others,
Among these I always find you.

I am singing, Lord, I worship.
Raised hands hold my heart high
Which overflows with joy and admiration
in the knowledge of you.

I am shouting, Lord, in my worship,
Adamant of your power and strength.
People around know that I love you,
I am proud and exulted with praise.

It is quiet, Lord, and I worship you.

Sophie Inglis

22 God is, God is, in all we are -
God is, God is, so praise Him
From here until the furthest star -
God is, God is, so praise Him.
There is no bound to God's great love
No depths below nor heights above
The living of our lives shall prove
    God is, God is, so praise Him.

In all our knowledge, wisdom, power -
God is, God is, so praise Him.
In every creature, every flower -
God is, God is, so praise Him.
In air and sea and warm sun rays
Our seconds, minutes, hours and days.
Wherever people give Him praise
    God is, God is, so praise Him.

In all our loved ones, parent, child -
God is, God is, so praise Him.
In all the folk who drive us wild -
God is, God is, so praise Him.
Where leaders of the world may meet
Where people and their neighbours speak
Where beggars sit beside the street.
    God is, God is, so praise Him.

In those who dare to live in faith -
God is, God is, so praise Him.
In pilgrims not afraid of death -
God is, God is, so praise Him.
In sharing love instead of fear
In spreading joy instead of tears
In making peace and justice here,
    God is, God is, so praise Him.

We know that as we travel on -
God is, God is, so praise Him.
In Jesus Christ his risen Son -
God is, God is, so praise Him.
In all our actions, every prayer,
In bread and wine together shared,
Wherever Christians show they care.
    God is, God is, so praise Him.

Colin Ferguson

23   Haiku

Poets paint with words
An artist paints with a brush
God painted mankind

Peter Morriss

24

Made in God's image
Pure imagination
Given to me
Given to you
Single light
Brightest light
When given is mirrored
Multiplied brightness
Encircles us now.

Deborah M McVey

25 Fruitful

My love for you comes with joy
The joy that comes from your peace
The peace that teaches patience
The patience that is kind
The kindness that breeds good
The good that fosters trust
The trust that lies gently
The gentleness of firm self -control
The control of my love for you....

Melanie Smith

26

Lord
it does not matter
whether our congregation
is large or small,
we are excited and joyful
because we meet
in the name of Jesus.

Whisper your word
through the noise and silence
of our worship,
to each one present.

Then,
it will not matter
whether our task is overwhelming
or the crowds outside unheeding,
we will be obedient and hopeful
because we go in the name of Jesus.

Tony Burnham

27   Words

What words on this page
Can ever state my love for you?
What words can I say
To let the world know of you?
What words can I pray
To ever ask for things from you?
What words can I hear
To understand the size of you?
What words do I know
To thank you for the gift of you?
What words can I write
To explain my thoughts to you?

Words of love.
Words of wisdom.
Words of prayer.
Words of greatness.
Words of humility.
Words written to worship you.

Melanie Smith

28 On the way to Iona

Utter beauty....
Another bright and shining manifestation of God:
Hills, gloriously caparisoned in glowing gorse,
Or swathed in lustrous folds of burnished grass;
The young, fresh innocence of lambs;
The newly planted firs;
And deep, dark water....
So still....   So deep....

Deep as the borehole which Your Beauty sinks
Into the centre of my being,
Striking and liberating
The pent-up oil of praise!
At every bend Beauty flings wide her arms,
Exultant, laughing aloud her delight in You.

I have *seen* Beauty many times -
Now I *know* her -
She is Yours....   She is You!

June Plaice

45

29 Taste the bitter herbs of Passover and eat to make us fit:
Fit to travel across an unknown desert's sand,
Fit to seek a promised land,
Where humankind and God shall fully live.
For God does love and does forgive
Those who really share His feast.

Drink of the Christ wine,
for what we drink is from blood and tears.
Tears shed for those who die alone,
Tears shed when people cannot own
The Hope and Faith he freely gives.
For God does love and does forgive
Those who really share His feast.

Eat of the Christ bread,
for what we eat is broken heart and soul,
Hung on a cross because of love's great need.
To heal the sick, to help the hungry feed,
To free, give hope, to let all people live.
For God does love and does forgive
Those who really share His feast.

Feed on the Christ food,
for what we taste is life in all its fulness.
Life wholly given, life that is meant to share,
Life spent and bent in service and in prayer,
Life consumed in everything we give
To God who loves and does forgive
Those who really share His feast.

Colin Ferguson

30 Praise to you, Father almighty, who have made heaven and earth and have never left yourself without witness among your creatures.

Praise to you, eternal Son, Jesus Christ, who are the Father's word actually made flesh and setting up home in our midst.

Praise to you, holy Spirit, who are the ground and principle of all life, the kindler of faith, the source of hope, the foundation of love and of everything that is pure and true and holy and right.

Three-personed God, you are one in being, one in goodwill towards us, one in pardoning and peace-giving. In returning to you we are freed from what enslaves us and given strength to bear what distresses us.

Let your word among us today not return to you fruitless but get through our deafness and accomplish the purpose you have for us now.

Caryl Micklem

31 Lord of eternity, we adore you because you are also Lord of time and space, God of every day.

When we enjoy the beauty of a fine morning, it is your beauty that is beckoning to our hearts. When we pause to consider our ways, to attend to the voice of conscience, to be humbled by the example of great men and women, to take a wider look at life than the rush and hassle of ordinary days allow, it is you who are calling to us, you who are opening our eyes, you who are shaming us for our self-importance and self-centredness, you who are offering us forgiveness and renewal, a chance once again to make of time and space the ante-chamber of our real destiny and the proving-ground of our real stature.

As you recall us to right paths, so open up to us new opportunities in well-doing: and by your divine life offered to us, nourish and strengthen our humanity to serve your purpose within our daily circumstances. Through him who was not ashamed to call us his sisters and brothers, Jesus Christ our Lord.

Caryl Micklem

32 Elementary God

God of Earth, sustain us.
God of Wind, breathe life into us.
God of Fire, ignite us to action.
God of Water, refresh us, empower us.

God, Creator of the Elements,
Use us as elements of You.

Lesley Trenkel

33 The Singing Bread

The singing bread,
The laughing wine;
What joyous ecstasy is mine.

The song is hushed....
The laughter stills...
The peace of Love flows where it wills.

June Plaice

34   God in us

God,
You give the best hugs.
You have the broadest shoulders.
Your hands are so gentle.
Your eyes show real understanding.
Your smile is the warmest I know.
Your laugh sets others laughing.

Thank you for living in and through us.
Help us to sense you in us.
Help us to see you in others.

God,
You are the most tearful.
Your eyes show your deep pain.
Your face drops with disappointment.
You are the most depressed.
Your body is beaten and abused.
Your cheeks are reddened with anger.

Thank you for living in and through us.
Help us to sense you within us.
Help us to see you in others.

Lesley Trenkel

35 The Lord of Life

Jesus was born here on our earth
To show us God with a human face.
Jesus came to share our birth
Bringing light to the human race.

The Lord of Heaven, he comes to us,
A simple babe in a stable born.
The Lord of Love, he lives in us,
Our Saviour God, this Christmas morn.

The Lord of Life, Emmanuel,
God with us, as a lowly king,
The Prince of Peace, the mighty God,
Christ is born, His praises sing.

Colin and Carol Dixon

36

A star -
why a star?
Remote, afar, constant
Link with time eternal, God's future
Wondrous galaxies too great to comprehend
Creator of all,
We adore.

A star -
Why a star?
Miraculously grasped
Held within each human frame
Radiance of God now shining outwards
Reaching, by it's energy co-creating
We adore.

Deborah M McVey

37
Rock-a-bye baby in Jesse's tree,
A glorious sign your birth shall be,
The flow'ring of the tree of life
That draws the nations from their strife.

Rock-a-bye baby, where you rest
The peaceful dove has built her nest,
And star and candle through the night
Lead those who seek your unquenched light.

Rock-a-bye baby in Jesse's tree,
The bough must break to set men free,
But from the stump new flowers will grow
And branches with new light will glow.

Gwen Patterson

 38 # Water into Wine

Alone . . . .
Gone!
Why?
Die.

Around . . . .
Found.
Give
Live.

John Dean

39 He is risen, He is risen
(1 Corinthians 15)

Listen to the message which was given to you -
The Good News of our Lord Christ,
Hear now once again the word you first received
And on which your faith stands firm:

He is risen, He is risen

If it was for nothing that you first believed
Jesus Christ died for our sins,
Now recall how he was raised to life again,
And He lives that we might live (in him).

He is risen, He is risen, Alleluia, He is Lord,
He is risen, He is risen, Alleluia, He is Lord.

Now to Him who gives us more than we can dream,
Only God whom we adore,
Jesus Christ our Lord, who died for all our sins,
Glory now and evermore.

He is risen, He is risen, Alleluia, He is Lord,
He is risen, He is risen, Alleluia, He is Lord (of all)

Simon Dixon

40   My Light and my Salvation
(Psalm 27 v.1)

Imagine: You walk alone at night, pass the cemetery, down the short cut through the fields - complete silence and darkness - would you think of this text then?

Imagine: You are alone at home and there is a power cut would you remember this text then?

Nothing is different except the darkness: that's why we are afraid. In daylight, we think nothing can happen to us when we are alone. Light takes away our fears. Think of the time when you were a little child and you had a little orange light that made you feel at ease so you could fall asleep. God says He's our light; He can take away our dark worries and fears. God as a light gives us hope and confidence that things will work out right or that we can turn to Him for comfort if they don't, in the way that the lights of home give us hope and comfort after a walk in the dark. When we light candles we tell others how we hope that they will see these lights and get their hopes back. This is one of the reasons for carrying lights when people are walking in a protest march against right extremism and racism. Even the smallest light can make the darkness disappear.

"The light shines in the darkness, and the darkness has never put it out".

John 1.5:

A small candle can destroy the darkness but the darkness can never destroy the light of a small candle.

Even when the darkness in our lives seems to be invincible, and tries to destroy all our hope, we can be sure that God's light and our hope through that light, is with us.

With this hope we can be lights lit by God for others in the darkness of fear and sorrow.

Antje Brunotte and
Beatrijs Boersema

41   **Candlelight**

Here I am,
Flickering among you.
Never still, not even for a minute.
In the night you look to me, you need me,
To guide you through the darkness,
To lead you from trouble.
In the daytime you forget all about me.
You shut me out.
But I'm still there.
The eager spark if you need encouragement,
The gentle glow if you need the warmth of a friend.
You might forget all about me,
But I'm always burning my flame....
For you.

Rebekah Slow

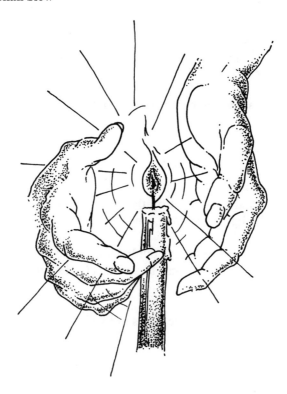

42 Have you ever woken up early on a dark winter morning, and struggled to find your clothes in the blackness because the light would be just too much for your eyes? You never get matching socks! You end up with your sweater on back to front! It's impossible to get it right without the light.

Play "Blindman's Buff". You suddenly you hear a sound. You move towards it when a laugh crackles behind you. You turn round to catch the person but end up flat on your back with your legs tangled around the nearest chair!

Darkness causes confusion, chaos even. With no clear direction you end up just moving round in circles.

This is how I see light; as a guide, as something to show us what's going on, something to navigate by. Sailors used to use the stars to get from one place to another.

Jesus said: I am the light of the world (John 8.12), Whoever follows me will have the light of life and never walk in darkness. He offers us a guide through life; an end to the chaos and confusion of people, and a chance for us to get it right.

Back to that original dark morning. It's black. It's freezing. You're comfortable in your warm bed and your eyes are accustomed to the gloom. The light would be just too much! Maybe sometimes Jesus' light is just too much. We're too complacent in our cosy, little, blind ways.

Open your eyes! Turn on the light, and let Jesus in.

Charlotte Atkinson

43 How can I see you in this place?
How can my life reflect your grace?
Maybe I can see you in my new friends' face.
Can they love you Lord?
Bleak was my life 'till I found you
Without a meaning my heart grew.
Once I got to know you, you made my life anew,
Now I love you Lord.

Vicky Harris

44   Flower Fragrance

Green hearted winter snowdrop,
symbol of God's renewing love,
turn your face to the sun,
as the days lengthen
and He sets his face to go to Jerusalem.

Pale yellow hosanna trumpet of spring,
accompany Him on His journey,
and as your shining petals brighten our day,
help us to sense His presence in our darkness,
His suffering in the agony of the world.

Flower fragrance of anointed love,
fill our house, our hearts, our world,
with the life giving news of Easter.

Kate McIlhagga

45   If

God said
I AM.
But it was not enough,
Man added just one little word
Having two letters:
If.

If God...
If man...
If we believe
If we obey
If such and such and this and that...

A little word,
But generation after generation strives
And fails
To plumb its meaning,
Having determined that this riddle must be solved
Before we come to God.

But God says only this:
I AM.
I am the life that drives you forward
I am the death that you must die
I am the source, the way, the end
There is nothing that is not Mine.
I am there in your solitude
And when you meet together.
I am in the stillness
And in all that flows
I AM
And you are Mine
Therefore worship Me.

W S Beattie

46 How can the worship of this congregation
achieve rapture and joy
in response to your glory and grace?

How can such feeble creatures
echo the alleluias
of the saints
in heaven?

Holy Spirit
come to us
and set alight our blighted offering;
fan the flames with your wind
and refine us in the heat of your presence.

Let our hymns swing,
our prayers be passionate
and our words enthusiastic.
Then your people will shout their praise
in unison with the throng
crowding the throne
and, like true citizens of heaven,
look to Jesus and say
Amen.

Tony Burnham

47 Who am I, holy God,
          to come near
          to your glory?

Who am I, almighty God
        to glimpse
        your splendour?

Who am I, welcoming God,
        to share your fire,
        to walk your mountain,
        to hear your voice?

Yet, in Jesus your Son,
you draw me to yourself
in wonder and in awe
and
before my very eyes
heaven is earthed.

Thank you, dear God
for understanding my need
to experience the heights
and witness the mystery of your presence on earth.

Thank you for moments in my life
when the light of your presence
has lifted my spirits
and strengthened my flagging faith.

But thank you, too,
for not allowing me to hide in the cloud
and for leading me down again
to face the cries of the world,
meeting its pain with your power.

David Jenkins

48   Creation

Views from a hill
Across a valley
Bustling town.
Turn to the hills,
See God's amazing creation
Hear the birds singing and wind blowing
Feel the rain.

I moved on from the hill, on through a wood,
And down to a stream.
I could hear the birds singing
And see the fish swimming.
They saw me and fled
But they didn't know me.

The rain started falling down from the sky
I could feel the rain
I could smell the rain.

The people didn't see me
The creatures didn't know me
but God sees me
and God knows me.

Anon

49 Supermarkets appear at roundabouts;
modern temples to greed.
On Sundays now, the ever faithful
Pilgrims come to honour their god.
Trolleys without direction,
empty become filled
as the Pilgrims meditate
over what they should buy.
Priests at the checkout
bless goods with electronic bleeps;
the Pilgrims pay homage with plastic
and leave.
It's a pity for some
that God can't be bought in
Supermarkets.

Pamela Harvey

50   The Sermon Song   (sung to "Men of Harlech")

Can you hear? The pews are creaking,
And the minister is speaking,
But he might as well be squeaking
For the sound we hear.
Summer colds and winter sneezes
Might be signs of dread diseases,
And a deacon, if you please, is
Coughing in my ear-

Please try not to shuffle
Your feet, or to snuffle,
This week's text
Might be like next
Week's: for the details you've contrived to muffle,
Do not whisper.
Eat your crisps or
Kick around your handbag,
Hit your sister.
Has the preacher such a lisp, or
Is that your false teeth?

For all I know, this week's sermon
Could be couched in French or German
Prove that when God made the firma-
ment it was royal blue.
I don't think it's quite that boring,
But someone behind me's snoring
And we're totally ignoring
Her: we've been there too.

Don't drop your collection,
Unwrap your confection-
ery so
we do not know
And identify the sound by its direction
The oration's
Peroration
Might be a doctrinal
Innovation,
But we're lacking information -
Here's the final hymn.

J M Low

Prayer

I know, Lord, that you are all-powerful;
     that you can do everything your want.
You ask how I dare question your wisdom
     when I am so very ignorant.
I talked about things I did not understand,
     about marvels too great for me to know.
You told me to listen while you spoke
     and to try to answer your questions.
In the past I knew only what others had told me,
     but now I have seen you with my own eyes.
So I am ashamed of all I have said
     and repent in dust and ashes.

Job 42.2-6

May the Lord Himself, who is our source of peace, give you peace at all times
and in every way. The Lord be with you all.

2 Thessalonians 3.16

Shout for joy to the Lords, all the world!
Worship the Lord with joy;
come before him with happy songs.
Acknowledge that the Lord is God.
He made us, and we belong to him.
we are his people, we are his flock.

Enter the temple gates with thanksgiving
go into its courts with praise;
Give thanks to him and praise him.
for the Lord is good his love is eternal;
and his faithfulness last for ever.

Psalm 100

When in obedience to the Lord's command his people show forth his sacrifice on the cross by the bread broken and the wine outpoured for them to eat and drink, he himself, risen and ascended, is present and gives himself to them for their spiritual nourishment and growth in grace. United with him and with the whole Church on earth and in heaven his people gathered at his table present their sacrifice of thanksgiving and renew the offering of themselves, and rejoice in the promise of his coming in glory.

URC Manual p.5; para 15

The Lord Jesus Christ continues his ministry in and through the Church, the whole people of God called and committed to his service and equipped by him for it. This service is given by worship, prayer, proclamation of the Gospel, and Christian witness;

URC Manual p.7; para 19

51 The Voice of my Lord

"Be with me" I whispered, as the sun began to rise
"I am here" He answered, "I am by your side".

"Be with me" I whispered, "when I have your work to do"
"I am here" He answered, "I am here with you".

"Be with me" I whispered, "for I sometimes feel alone"
"I am here" He answered, "you are never on your own".

"Be with me" I whispered, "when I have a load to bear"
"I am here" He answered, "I am always there".

"Be with me" I whispered, "when I feel I have to grieve"
"I am here" He answered, "I will never leave".

"Be with me" I whispered, "may we never part"
"I am here" He answered, "I am dwelling in your heart".

Claire Seal

52 It's a way to strengthen your faith
It's a means of receiving your grace
Meeting new friends, singing new songs
Get away from everything.

Think of his prayer in solitude
Elijah in a land he never knew
John the Baptist in the wilderness
Get away from everything.

Dawn (Jamaica)

53 Early morning about six
Don't know what to think
Feeling cold as the wind blew
Trees are clouded with morning dew
Where else is there such a place?
So peaceful, lovely and lonely
With God in the midst.

Marcia McEwan

54 In the open wilderness
God is watching us
In the morning, in the noontime
And the evening too.

Michele Henry

55 In the name of Jesus the shepherd, we pray for all who wonder which way to turn next, or where their next meal is coming from.
May the church also be known as a reliable guide.

In the name of Jesus the guardian and lover of souls, we pray for all orphans of life's storms, and all who seek someone who will love them for themselves and not just for their usefulness or their looks or their money.
May the church also take real care, and not see people only as potential converts.

In the name of Jesus the friend of sinners, we pray for all whom the world passes by, afraid of involvement, afraid of contamination.
May the church also stretch out the hand of friendship and reconciliation wherever it can.

In the name of Jesus the prophet, we pray for all who need to hear a voice of summons, of challenge and of hope in the midst of life's disappointments and despairs.
May the church also never cease to be prophetic, telling what it knows however much this may be resented.

In the name of Jesus the priest and king, we pray for all who feel blocked off from God, or who, in any pain or distress, need the anointing presence of one with healing power.
May the church also play its part in the heavenly work of making people whole, and of giving a new cohesion to communities ruptured by conflicting loyalties.

Caryl Micklem

56 My desire for you,
O God,
is great.
May it always be so.

Natasha Winter

57 God, where is your Spirit,
The helper, guide and friend?
He is here with us now,
Waiting patiently to be invited in.
Open our ears Lord,
Open our eyes,
Open our hearts
To let him in.
Let us not deny his presence
Or underestimate his power.

Natasha Winter

58 Nobody Noticed
(Matthew 25: 31-36)

Nobody noticed when you were born
    in a cold, draughty winter stable.
Forgive us, Lord, when we do not notice the homeless.
And we ask you to give us strength to help them.

Nobody noticed when you fought the temptation of evil
    in a hot, humid desert.
Forgive us, Lord, when we do not notice the build up to war.
And we ask you to help us to bring peace.

Nobody noticed when you helped individuals,
    the thieves and the prostitutes.
Forgive us, Lord, when we do not notice how we avoid "bad" people
And help us to carry your torch into their lives.

Nobody noticed when you were hung on the cross
    hungry, beaten, betrayed.
Forgive us, Lord, when we do not notice the unfairness of our world.
And help us to fight for justice.

When the Day of Judgement comes
Notice us, Lord.
As we notice you
In the poor, the solder, the criminal and the prisoner of conscience.

Melanie Smith

59 Lord, you know me well.
You knew me before I was born.
You knew me before you created the world.
I am in your plan.

You tell me, "Who can add a single hour
To his life by worrying?"
You tell me, "Be strong and of good courage
Do not be afraid, nor dismayed"
I am your concern.

You say "Love me as I love you".
You love each one of us with your whole being,
And you forgive us when we are sorry,
When we want to do your will,
But something stops us.
I am your child.

You changed my life,
You know me,
You protect me,
You guide me,
You help me,
You love me.

Thank you.

Carol Moore

60 **Psalm 139**

Lord,
You know all about me
Wherever I am
You're always with me.

Lord,
You know everything I do
Wherever I go
You're always beside me.

And Lord,
You even knew me
When you were creating me
Before I was born.
And Lord,
You'd still be there with me,
In the darkness of night
You're always there for me.

Lord,
I want to know all about you
You are my protector
From all that is evil.
Lord,
I want to be like you.
Your greatness astounds me.
You reign forever.

Lynn Cockerham

61   Finding Out

I've said it before now I'll say it again
Sometimes I don't know my heart from my head.
What I can' t say and what I can' t see
Is someone who cares that much for me.
So please if you're listening don't get me wrong
I'm trying to be as honest as I can in this song.

Six years on and I know I believe
I live by the grace I fail to receive
And you're the only one who I know
Who really, really, really loves me so.

I can't find this peace of mind without you here
And can't see what it means to live in fear
I'm finding out.

You think to yourself oh please not me
I've carried this weight too long you'll see
But I know there's nothing else I'll find
That's worth living for in this life.

Stuart Turner and James Bott

62 When the day's beginning
is dark and grim
Lighten our darkness

When my heart thuds
from one fear to the next
Lighten my darkness

When the next task
seems insurmountable
Lighten our darkness

When my mind races
like a rat in a trap
Lighten my darkness

When all seems lost
over the "cliffs of fall" *
Lighten our darkness

O encompassing Love
be our shield and our companion
Calm us as you stilled the storm
Enfold us in your loving arm
Encourage us to pilgrim with you
and surround us always
with the halo of your presence

Kate McIlhagga

* Gerard Manley Hopkins

63 Father

Father, we know that you're here,
Be with us as we draw near.
Open our hearts and our eyes,
Help us reach to the skies

We know we can do anything with you
We'll go anywhere you lead us to.

As we find answers through our prayers
Use our lives and all we'll share.
Receive from us all our praise;
All our blemishes erase.

We know we can do anything with you
We'll go anywhere you lead us to.

Now as we close our eyes
Take control of our lives,
All we do and say
Take our own thoughts away.

Stuart Turner and James Bott

64 All on my own

If I were God for a day, what would I do?
Would I keep things as they are or start anew?
And if I started afresh, could I follow it through
All on my own?

If I were God, would I banish starvation,
Would I stop nation fighting nation,
And could I live up to this obligation,
All on my own?

If I were God, could I put the world to right,
could I give the sick good health and the blind sight,
when I can't show the Way, the Truth and the Light
All on my own?

Don't be like Thomas, with so much doubt,
of never believing, without a shout,
of "it's not fair! I wasn't there!"
And "Don't ask me, 'cos I can't see
All on my own".

If I were God would I help us to understand
that with Him, help is always at hand.
And now I need no longer stand
All on my own?

No.   If I were offered the job, I'd refuse.
For I know that with Him the world can't lose.
And anyway, how could I choose
All on my own?

Nicholas Clark

65 Thank you for friends
And all they have done;
The knowledge they bring
Of you and your Son.
The laughter and tears,
The giving and growing,
Our communication,
Love sharing and showing.
Like dust in the breeze
Without you we're naught
Yet into your kingdom
Through you we're brought.
May we all get home safely
And walk in your way
Telling people of you
In all that we say.

Susanne Rook

66 I dream of a church
(could be sung to "The Cowboy's Lament")

I dream of a church that joins in with God's laughing
as she rocks in her rapture, enjoying her art:
she's glad of her world, in its risking and growing:
'tis the child she has borne and holds close to her heart.

I dream of a church that joins with God's weeping
as she crouches, weighed down by the sorrow she sees:
as she cries for the hostile, the cold and no-hoping -
for she bears in herself our despair and dis-ease.

I dream of a church that joins in with God's dancing
as she moves like the wind and the wave and the fire:
a church that can pick up its skirts, pirouetting,
with steps that can signal God's deepest desire.

I dream of a church that joins in with God's loving
as she bends to embrace the unlovely and lost:
a church that can free, by it's sharing and daring,
the imprisoned and poor - and then shoulder the cost.

God, make us a church that joins in with your living,
as you cherish and challenge, reign in and release,
a church that is winsome, impassioned, inspiring:
lioness of your justice, and lamb of your peace.

Kate Compston

67 Meditation

Lord,
Help us use our time and talents
To your advantage.
Help us to praise and glorify your name
In witness to others.

As we stand in the face of adversity
Help us overcome our fears
And guide us in our search for a
prayerful life of worship to your holy name.

In gladness, help us remember our friends
Who suffer as we smile.
In sadness, warm our hearts to the
Love that surrounds us-

In our lives, help us to mirror
The goodness of your Son, Jesus,
And in death, guide us to serve
At your right hand.

In everything we do, help us to
Live to be worthy of being your servants
And guide our singing, dancing and prayer
To praise your holy name.

As you love us, we love you,
In memorable thanks for your goodness.
In reverence of your greatness
Lord we praise you.

Amen.

Emma Thornton

68 Ansafone

"After the bleep
you may speak
and leave a message. .."

Suddenly my mind goes blank.
I pull myself together,
hurriedly summon up
a garbled precis
and deliver it self-consciously
into the void.

Not so with prayers -
there is this feeling
they are heard at once,
not queuing messages
for a celestial Ansafone,
but instant delivery
faster than thought;
and deeper still
an understanding -
that even if an answer
isn't phoned back
straight away,
ultimate answers there will be:

sometimes much later
from a broader view,
often through opportunities,
practically always -
in completely unexpected ways.

Cecily Taylor

69 Living God,
We praise you for the wonder of your creation,
For the beautiful and frightening pattern of life
        formed through your power and love.
Your touch is revealed to us in the tiniest particle
        of an atom, and the glory of the universe.
You have shown yourself to us as the Creator:
Thank you for the life you give.

We praise you for the wonder of your salvation,
For coming amongst us in Jesus Christ.
In him your love became someone we can recognise.
His challenging words brought hope and healing.
On the cross he revealed the depth of your commitment to us.
Through his resurrection sin and death lost their power.
You have shown yourself to us as the Saviour:
Thank you for the life you give.

We praise you for the wonder of your new life,
Your Spirit comes to teach and inspire.
As we grow in fellowship and faith we feel
        the Spirit's prompting.
When we are slow or fearful we sense the Spirit's challenge.
You have shown yourself to us as the Sustainer:
Thank you for the life you give.

Neil Thorogood

70 Different

I know I said things would be different
But really I knew it never would be;
Somehow I'd try to make you happy,
I can't explain what comes naturally.
I know I've let you down again.
Lord when will I find the piece that's missing?
I know because I've played this role before,
There must be a part of me not giving
But I know I'll keep knocking on your door.

Stuart Turner and James Bott

71 Come among us Living Lord.

Come among us living Lord,
We come to hear your living word
We meet together in the name of Christ
To share your mission and your sacrifice;
To receive the power which only you can give -
That we might live!
Come fill this time of silence.

Martin John Nicholls

72 Lord, you gave us hands to use,
To mould and do the things for you,
For touching, loving, helping hands
We thank you Lord for these.

The voices you gave to sing your praise
And help to spread your name.
For saying the way that we feel
And giving the comfort in times of need.

Our eyes you gave to us to see
The wonders of the world.
To use for those that need our help,
we give you thanks for all of these.

Wendy Manners

73 Remember Me

Have not you remembered me
From when you were young?
I knew you before you were born
And I love you just as much now
As I did then.
Will you come to me and
Trust me with your life?
I will be your everlasting Father
And your rock in times of trouble.
I will be your helper, protector,
Healer, provider - but only if you let me.
I want you to choose me but even
if you don' t I still love you
because I'm your friend.
Listen to me for I want to give
you many gifts you may never
have had before now.
Trust me and follow me.
Love from your friend   -   Jesus.

Kate Gray

74 Since September Unemployed

There are so many questions, Lord,
That I must ask of you,
The hope I have for my life,
Where am I going to?

What do the people think, Lord,
When they look at me?
Am I who I think I am,
Who is it that they see?

Do they see a failure, Lord,
One more scrounger on the dole?
Or a worker fighting for success,
Just searching for my role?

There are so many questions, Lord,
That I must ask of you.
And does it really matter, Lord,
Who I am, to them or you?

Melanie Smith

75   Prayer

Everything within your life,
take to the Lord in prayer,
from "Why do people die in wars?"
to "please stop that squeaking stair!"

Sophie Inglis

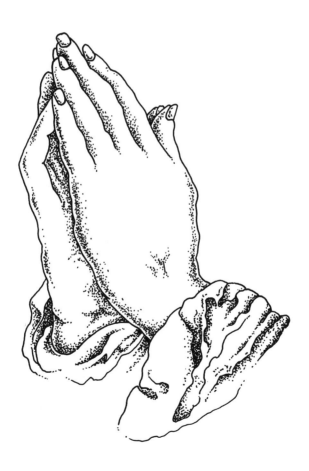

76

Spoken by a 35-45 year old:

> He never reached my age:
> thirty when he died, or thereabouts,
> yet in his brief, tumultuous years
> he knew grief greater far than I have known,
> felt pain beyond my bearing,
> joy deeper than the depths of my delight,
> and knew his Father in it all.
>> Come, Lord Jesus!
>> Speak to my time.
>> Receive the worship of my wondering love.

Spoken by someone over 70:

> The years have sped to bring me to my time,
> now more than twice the age at which he died,
> and yet with less than half the inner peace he knew.
>> Come Lord Jesus!
>> Speak to my time.
>> Receive the worship of my wondering love.

Spoken by someone in their twenties:

> Though still yet young
> The years divide me from his cradle birth.
> As infant child he nestles in my heart,
> as teacher still excites my mind to thought,
> as dying Lord he brings me to my knees,
> and rising, lifts me far beyond myself.
>> Come, Lord Jesus!
>> Speak to my time.
>> Receive the worship of my wondering love.

Spoken by a teenager:

> Full strong, I serve him in my growing years,
> He calls, I follow, and the way is clear,
> though I must trace his footsteps in the sand
> and all my strength is weakness when I sense his power.
>> Come, Lord Jesus!
>> Speak to my time.
>> Receive the worship of my wondering love.

Spoken by a child:

> And he was once like me;
> hand-held in Mary's love,
> turning to Joseph for advice,
> and daily running to and from his school.
> Once like me, may I grow on to be like him.
> > Come, Lord Jesus!
> > Speak to my time.
> > Receive the worship of my wondering love.

Donald Hilton

Jesus looked round and saw rich men dropping their gifts in the temple treasury, and he also saw a very poor widow dropping in two little copper coins. He said, "I tell you that this poor widow put in more than all the others. For the others offered their gifts from what they had to spare of their riches; but she, poor as she is, gave all she had to live on."

Luke 21 v.1-4

Jesus and his disciples were at supper. The Devil had already put into the heart of Judas, the son of Simon Iscariot, the thought of betraying Jesus. Jesus knew that the Father had given him complete power; he knew that he had come from God and was going to God. So he rose from the table, took off his outer garment, and tied a towel round his waist. Then he poured some water into a basin and began to wash the disciples' feet and dry them with the towel round his waist.

John 13 v.2-5

The attitude you should have is the one that Christ Jesus had:
He always had the nature of God, but he did not think that by
     force he should try to become equal with God.
Instead of this, of his own free will he gave up all he had,
     and took the nature of a servant.
He became like man and appeared in human likeness.
He was humble and walked the path of obedience all the way to
     death - his death on the cross.
For this reason God raised him to the highest place above and
     gave him the name that is greater than any other name.
And so, in honour of the name of Jesus all beings in heaven,
     on earth, and in the world below will fall on their knees,
and all will openly proclaim that Jesus Christ is Lord, to
     the glory of God the Father.

Philippians 2 v.5-11

Are zeal for the glory of God, love for the Lord Jesus Christ and a desire for the salvation of the world, so far as you know your own heart, the chief motives which lead you to enter this ministry?

Do you promise to fulfil the duties of your charge with all fidelity, to lead your people in worship, to preach the Word and administer the sacraments, to exercise pastoral care and oversight, and to give leadership to the Church in its mission to the world?

URC Manual; Schedule C

The United Reformed Church acknowledges that the life of faith to which it is called is a gift of the Holy Spirit continually received in Word and Sacrament and in the common life of God's people.

URC Manual; Schedule D

I worship, Lord,
In many ways
In dance
In prayer
With praise.

But what is it, Lord
That I must give
To breathe
To sing
To live.

Don't tell me, Lord,
I know the way
To give
To you
Today.

I must give, Lord,
Just all of me,
To know
I know
I'm free.

Melanie Smith

78 Bounty

In my pocket
I keep four jagged pieces
of coloured paper.
A child who has just learnt
to use scissors
gave them to me.

As I was leaving
he lent towards me
with the air of a Maharaja
bestowing half a kingdom.
"You have these now" he said
"From me!"
And I treasure them
in equal measure.

Cecily Taylor

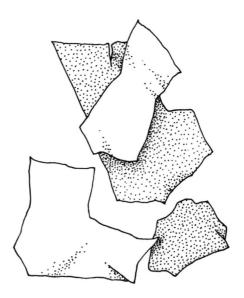

79 Michael

He was my friend
He is my friend
Was I his friend?

He gave to me
He gives to me
What gave I to him?

He had so much
He has so much
What do I have now?

He smiled at life
He smiles hereafter
What smiles can I share?

Melanie Smith

80   Giving your gifts - A job for life

To the church:

You say you need people to work
Within the Church. You need
A secretary, treasurer, church leaders and youth leaders.
But do people dare volunteer
Because they fear a
Job for life?

The church has many things
to do to keep it going
and make it strong.
Parties, outings, pantomimes,
church dinners, uniformed
organisations, church
holidays, but who does
it fall on? The
Same few who
are prepared to help
and give their life.

To God:-

Lord, when we look into our lives
Guide us to do what you want
of us using the skills that
each individual has.

Many have many skills
And use them within the church,
But when we have carried
out our responsibility for
a number of years let
Somebody take them off
our hands.

Let us carry these out
while we are enthusiastic and keen
not because we are bored or fed up.

A B Royal

81 Memories of Sychar
(John4.1-41)

I barely even saw his face,
All I remember is the grace.
When he turned to say "good-bye",
I knew, to save my life, he'd die.

I think back on the smile he gave,
When he said I was no more a slave.
He proclaimed freedom for me,
Promised great riches in heaven I'd see.

I asked him what price I must pay,
To be forgiven in such a way.
The price, he said, is too high to count,
Life is worth more than any amount.

What then, I asked, shall I give,
In what way should I live?
All of me, he then asked for,
Only my heart can open the door.

And so I gave my love to him,
For eternal life to win.
And as he turned to say "good-bye",
I knew, to save my life, he'd die.

Melanie Smith

82 Full House

Nearly out of wine,
Pots still in the sink,
Cooking since dawn,
And still can't sit down.
Where's that husband of mine?
               No time for traveller's tales!
               Get into that cellar!
               Bring more wine!

Now what's this?
More travellers seeking room.
That's a joke!
          Bathrooms full,
          Four on the snooker table,
          And now two more,
          Or nearly three if I can see aright.
          Still, can't be done,
               Husband! Tell them no room!
               Full House!
               Bingo!

But look at the man,
Crumbling with despair.
Hard working poor I'd say:
          rough hand,
          clean clothes,
          but patch on patch.
And she so young,
Time nearly due,
Vulnerable.
This Government!
To make a lass in her condition travel
Just to be counted!
She counts for nothing
And neither do we.
Even the beast's all bones and ears,
Worn out.

The stable! That's the answer!
Boarded up cave, really,
To shelter ox and ass.
At least the straw's clean.
Quieter than the pub.
The donkey can gossip with the ass!
Catch up on news.

Full House, the sign says.
No vacancies
        No room for compassion?
        A vacant heart
        And love denied?

History may condemn that stable lodging.
        No silken sheets,
        No midwife care,
        No tender care.
But in my heart I gave them more.
They left the stable
And the house.
Fled to Egypt
And from Herod's wrath
But never left my heart.

Y Mochyn Daear (adpt. Donald Hilton)

83
As I lay in silence
All I hear is peace
The stillness of the night
The laughter of the wind as it tickles the leaves
The lullaby of the birds slips gently into our minds,
Soothing our thoughts and easing our pains.

The sounds of heavy breathing surrounds us
All is silence,
All is at peace.

The window bears another vision, one of trees and fields
A natural earth that gives birth to beauty, colour and expression.
The songs of the people can be heard throughout the land.
They show no hatred only express joy and gaiety.
All tell stories which lie imbedded deep within their souls.
Songs which reflect feeling recognition of the one true God.

But something lurks like a dark cloud behind this festivity.
And is hidden beneath these sounds of joy.
It covers our first impressions
And poisons our foremost thoughts.
Our beliefs then become trivial
To the reality of these people.

We know no true poverty
We feel no true pain.
But we all share one vision, hope and true faith
Together we can make this land no longer a strange place.
No longer a foreign country.

Eternal rest will be present and,
All will be silence
All will be at peace.

Lorraine Downer

84 Reject

I wonder, is God like His Church?
They said, please in your gardens search
For things to bring
As offering
Next Sunday, for the harvest festival.

And so we did, though it was hard.
Because of drought our crops were marred,
The ground was dry, the prize blooms dead.
We brought just what we had instead
To make our harvest festival.

And on the day the church was decked
Most tastefully. Who would expect
So rich a show? Yet most, we saw
Came out of shops. Piled on the floor
Outside, pathetic, withering,
The rejects of our offering,
Chosen with love, but not quite suitable
For such a special festival.

Our lives are like our flowers.
Parched soils and barren hours
Make it hard for us to find
What we suppose You have in mind.
If everything we have we bring
will You reject our offering
When at the last we one and all
Compose Your harvest festival?

The humblest flower that grows on earth
Is wonderful beyond all worth.
Who dares assert it must be priced,
Shop-labelled, "Bought by Jesus Christ"?

And when, upon our final day,
Things of earth must fall away,
What one of us, however low,
Will not have something fit to show?

Anon

85 Gift Day

Cor, blast, thass Gift Day agin. Reckon I'll hatta give them suthin.
Give ter this, give ter that, give ter this one, give ter that one. Everybody
oughter stand on their own two flat feet, same as me. I don't look fer no
handouts, nor shouldn't they. 'Course if it was suthing I really cared
about, or someone what mattered, thass different. Things yew oughts
do, thats one thing. Things you want to do, people you really care
about, thats another. Get yer caring right, an the rest will follow. Bound
to. No way you can stop it. Like thet pore old widow and her mite,
whatever that was. Suthin like one of them new fangled pieces, I
shouldn't wonder. Less'n the rakeoff the priests got from one pigeon
sold in the temple courtyard. But you know what the good Lord said
about them - and about her. She cared, you see, that's what mattered.

W S Beattie

86 Give and Take

All we have has come from God,
He gives, we eagerly take.
Yet all we have should be given back,
Used solely for his sake.

God gave us his greatest gift,
His one and only son.
We took all he had then gave him up,
So we must ensure his work is done.

"The more you give the more you get"
Is not the reason for giving.
If everyone gave for the sake of it,
Life would be more worth living.

Sophie Inglis

87 Hollytime, variegated

There are so many marvellous things to give.
But when it comes to it
A diary, some calendars,
A book perhaps,
A box or two of chocolates
And that's my list complete,
Except for charities and cards.

A present is importunate
It asks an awkward question:
Do you know me?
Have you noticed
I'm a person too,
A sort of person,
Trying, a little, sometimes.

So send a card
To show goodwill
With seasonable words
That do not say too much
(And then I write a letter on it!)
I love buying Christmas cards,
Far more than I require.
And then I wonder who to send them to.
Isn't it funny!

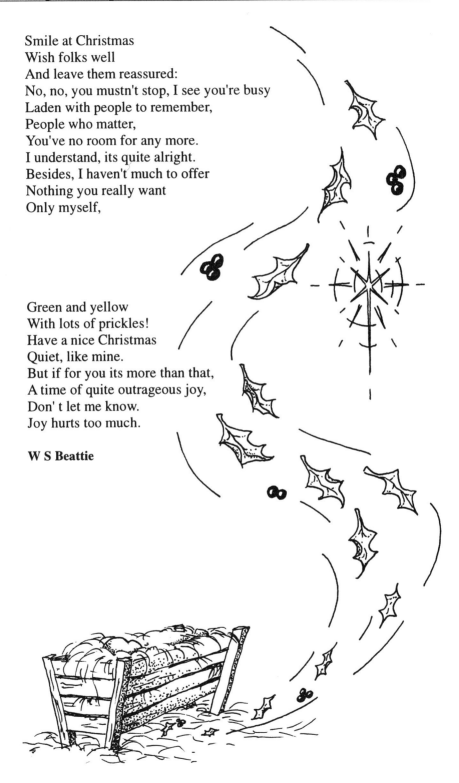

Smile at Christmas
Wish folks well
And leave them reassured:
No, no, you mustn't stop, I see you're busy
Laden with people to remember,
People who matter,
You've no room for any more.
I understand, its quite alright.
Besides, I haven't much to offer
Nothing you really want
Only myself,

Green and yellow
With lots of prickles!
Have a nice Christmas
Quiet, like mine.
But if for you its more than that,
A time of quite outrageous joy,
Don' t let me know.
Joy hurts too much.

W S Beattie

88 Lord God
you have never spurned or rejected
any gift offered
in love and sincerity.

Whether I have brought to you
a simple cry for help
or an elaborate act of praise
you have been equally receptive.

Help me not to be ashamed
of simple gifts.
Help me to be glad
of what skills I have
so they are used to your glory.

So may my worship
raise in praise to you
the routine experience
and the magic moments
of my life.

Lord,
I may not have
the great oratory of a preacher
or the sensitive touches of a poet;
I may not have
the vision of an artist
or the ear of a great musician
but I will strive to be
all that I ought to be
in your sight
and stretch my talents and skills
to the utmost
so that your world is filled with beauty
and my life becomes an offering of joy

David Jenkins

89 The Harvest is Rich

Look through his eyes, what do you see?
People in chains with a right to be free.
Lost and confused; wandering sheep;
too sad to laugh, too tired to weep.

> The harvest is rich but the labourers are few;
> there is so little time and so much left to do.
> The harvest is rich but the labourers are few,
> so pray to the Lord of the Harvest.

And with his ears, what do you hear?
Shouts of oppression; whispers of fear.
Cries of the hungry; words of the proud;
even the silence is shouting out loud!

> The harvest is rich but the labourers are few;
> there is so little time and so much left to do.
> The harvest is rich but the labourers are few,
> so pray to the Lord of the Harvest.

Come take his hand, what do you feel?
God's liberation; the power to heal;
power to break down the walls that we build,
freeing potential, as yet unfulfilled.

> The harvest is rich but the labourers are few;
> there is so little time and so much left to do.
> The harvest is rich but the labourers are few,
> so pray to the Lord of the Harvest.

Martin John Nicholls

90 The Given Life

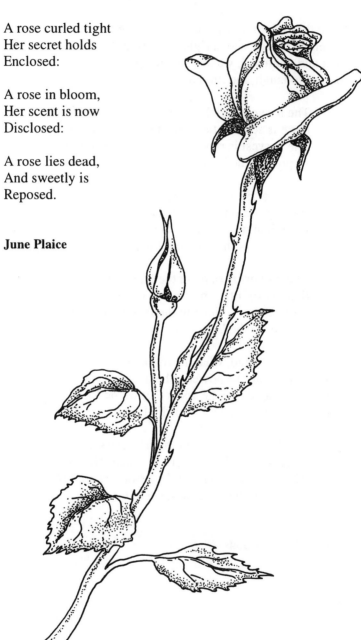

A rose curled tight
Her secret holds
Enclosed:

A rose in bloom,
Her scent is now
Disclosed:

A rose lies dead,
And sweetly is
Reposed.

June Plaice

91 The Breath of God

Tears are gently falling from the corners of my eyes,
I feel a bit embarrassed but no one seems surprised,
I try to wipe the droplets as they fall freely down my cheek,
But my heart is overflowing as I feel the One I seek.
My throat is choked with tears, I can hardly sing the song,
But my soul reflects the words and the meaning's just as strong.
"I need you dear Lord Jesus, and I long to feel your touch,
To feel the presence of the One I love so very much".
As these words are uttered, I feel a rushing through my soul,
My heart dilates in freedom as the barriers dissolve.
At last my soul lies open, uncluttered, crystal clear,
As I feel the breath of Jesus erase my hurt and fear.
My heart is crying harder than it's ever done before,
From relief, delight, emotion as He fills me more and more.
All my worries leave me, I feel Jesus by my side,
I can never doubt He loves me, in my heart He will abide.
Colours are exploding within my humble human frame,
With the power of Your Spirit Lord, I can never be the same.
Your loving gift is so strong that my heart will overflow,
May I use Your Spirit wisely so that others come to know,
How wondrous is your love dear God, how powerful Your Might,
How my life has changed Oh Lord, now You've filled my soul with light.

Claire Seal

As Jesus walked along the shore of Lake Galilee, he saw two fishermen, Simon and his brother Andrew, catching fish with a net. Jesus said to them, "Come with me, and I will teach you to catch men." At once they left their nets and went with him.

He went a little farther on and saw two other brothers, James and John, the sons of Zebedee. They were in their boat getting their nets ready. As soon as Jesus saw them, he called them; they left their father Zebedee in the boat with the hired men and went with Jesus.

Mark 1.16-20

In the church at Antioch there were some prophets and teachers: Barnabas, Simeon (called the Black), Lucius (from Cyrene), Manaen (who had been brought up with Herod the governor), and Saul. While they were serving the Lord and fasting, the Holy Spirit said to them, "Set apart for me Barnabas and Saul, to do the work to which I have called them."

They fasted and prayed, placed their hands on them, and sent them off.

Acts 13: 1-3

Christ is like a single body, which has many parts; it is still one body, even though it is made up of different parts. In the same way, all of us, whether Jews or Gentiles, whether slaves or free, have been baptised into the one body by the same Spirit, and we have all been given the one Spirit to drink.

For the body itself is not made up of only one part, but of many parts. If the foot were to say "Because I am not a hand, I don' t belong to the body," that would not keep it from being a part of the body. And if the ear were to say, "Because I am not an eye, I don' t belong to the body," that would not keep it from being a part of the body. If the whole body were just an eye, how could it hear? And if it were only an ear, how could it smell? As it is, however, God put every different part in the body just as he wanted it to be There would not be a body if it were all only one part! As it is, there are many parts but one body.

1 Corinthians 12: 12-20

Within the one, holy, catholic, apostolic Church the United Reformed Church acknowledges its responsibility under God:

— to live out, in joyful and sacrificial service to all in their various physical and spiritual needs, that ministry of caring, forgiving and healing love which Jesus Christ brought to all whom he met;
— and to bear witness.

URC Manual, p.4, para 11

The United Reformed Church gives thanks for the common life of the Church, wherein the people of God, being made members one of another, are called to love and serve one another and all people everywhere and to grow together in grace and in the knowledge of the Lord Jesus Christ. Participating in the common life of the Church within the local church, they enter into the life of the Church throughout the world. With that whole Church they also share in the life of the Church in all ages and in the communion of saints have fellowship with the Church triumphant.

URC Manual, p.6, para 16

I promise, in dependence on God's grace, to be faithful in private and public worship, to live in the fellowship of the Church and to share in its work, and to give and serve, as God enables me, for the advancement of his kingdom throughout the world.

URC Manual. Schedule A

92

A community creed

We believe in God,
In Jesus Christ,
In the Holy Spirit,
And in you and me.
We believe the Holy Spirit has freed us
To worship as a Community.
We believe the Holy Spirit works through
Balloons and ministers,
Daisies and wiggly children,
Clanging cymbals and silence,
Drama and the unexpected,
Choirs and banners,
Touching and praying,
Spontaneity and planning,
Faith and doubt,
Tears and laughter,
Leading and supporting,
Hugging and kneeling,
Dancing and stillness,
Applauding and giving,
Creativity and plodding,
Words and listening,
Holding and letting go,
Thank you and help me,
Scripture and alleluias,
Agonizing and celebrating,
Accepting and caring,
Through you and through me,
Through Love.
We believe God's Holy Spirit lives
in this community of dancing, hand-holding
people where lines of age and politics and
lifestyles are crossed.
We believe in praising God for life.
We believe in responding to God's grace
and love and justice for all people.
We believe in the poetry within each of us.
We believe in dreams and visions.
We believe in old people running and children leading.
We believe in the Kingdom of God within us.
We believe in Love.

Source unknown

93　Christmastide

In the moontime of the winter,
when the sun redly rises;
in the moontime of the winter,
when the trees starkly stretch,
then, 0 Christ, you come:
softly as a gently falling snowflake,
with the lusty energy of a newborn boy,
the blood and pain of your coming,
staining the distant horizon.

In the frost of the starlight,
when the sun gives way to moon,
in the frost of the starlight,
when the earth is turned to stone,
then, 0 Christ, you come:
slowly as the rhythm of the seasons,
quickly as the rush of cradling waters,
worshipped by the wise,
adored by the humble,
the ecstatic joy of your coming,
heralding songs of peace.

Into the world of refugee and soldier,
the soles of your feet have touched the ground.
Into the world of banker and beggar,
the soles of your feet have touched the ground.
Into the world of Jew and Arab,
the soles of your feet have touched the ground.

Walk with us saviour of the poor,
be a light on our way,
travel beside the weary,
fill the broken hearted with hope
and heal the nations,
that all may walk
in the light of the glory of God.

Kate McIlhagga

94 Not a distant God, but a God very near.
Not a silent God, but a God who has spoken.
Not a neutral or impassive God, but a God whose righteousness will prevail against all wrong, whose goodness will overcome evil, whose mercy will forgive sins and create in us a clean heart and a right spirit. This God and Father of our Lord Jesus Christ let us worship now with awe and with joy, ascribing to him alone all glory and thanksgiving for ever.

Caryl Micklem

95 Lord Jesus Christ, we adore you because you did not disdain to become one of us.
You share all that gives us joy and all that gives us pain.
You accompany us wherever we have to go.
You enlighten our ignorance; your strength makes up for our weakness; your forgivingness does away with our sins.

May we be enabled by the holy Spirit to make sincere confession of the mess we make of being human as you, Lord, are human; to accept the pain and inconvenience of true neighbourliness; and to grow day by day more like you, who have deigned to be made like us.

Caryl Micklem

96 We fall between the gaps we make.
Sometimes a bridge is built, but then,
Foundations insecure, and planks worked loose,
It falls.

Youth and age; that gap is clear:
How often does the youth club meet
The luncheon club for mid-day pensioners,
Darby and Joan, the Toddlers' Mums?
     Yet will not one day
     All youth find greying hair and stumbling tread?
     And were not ancient ones a teenage crowd:
     Noisy, fancy-free, and locked within themselves?

Black and white,
Pink, brown, and yellow,
Purple, if you please,
Or variegated crimson-blue.
Widen the gap! The colours are too bright!
     Yet shall we ever find the rainbow crock of gold,
     Without each other?

Men and women; women, men:
Uniting well in sex,
But not committees.
Unless they're pushed by mathematic rule
To find the statutory ones;
Create some fulcrum for uneasy balance.
     Yet who can tell which one the Spirit next will touch
     And truth engender?

A man once came, not quick to blame,
Not strident in his ways, but with God's truth ablaze,
More ready to be struck than strike.
The curtain tore in two,
And God met us, and Gentile, Jew.
A bridge was built,
And all the world was new.

But that was long ago.

Donald Hilton

97

So many bodies Lord, that you have taken for your own,
So many lives in which you've walked and worked and suffered,
So many paving-stones on which your blood is shed,
I name them Lord, in silence of communion.
Those in whose lives you lived and live superbly,
Those widely known and celebrated,
Those unknown but to you, and those who love them.
For their standing in your Way, not being moved,
Not giving in to mockery or fear,
Risking all for truth and love of others:
Yes, those who, even now, labelled as terrorists or fools,
Scorned, ignominious may yet in future times
Be recognised, or not, by men, but whose
Hearts are open to you, - whose motives pure,
I name them with you and you with them
That their despair of harvest may not overwhelm,
That their Gethsemane may not overcome -
And even to crucifixion, they stand firm -
However unimportant or ridiculous
The cause for which they suffer seems to others.
The world is overturned by so-called fools and knaves.

Gwen Patterson

98   Simon Peter's Song

The wind is blowing colder than ever before,
but the fear fear inside me chills me much more.
The light from the fire there has a welcoming glow
But no one must see me, no one must know..

I never knew him.

What's that you ask me? I don't understand.
You recognise me? You've got the wrong man!
Didn't you hear me? Are you doubting my word?
Me? Follow a man like him? It's really absurd!

I never knew him.

Please don' t ask me to repeat what I have said!
(I wish I had the courage to admit what's in my head).
But what difference would it make, the man's as good as dead. ...

    "Three times you' ll deny me before the dawn
    Three times you' ll disown me before the morn."
    He knows me better than I know my own mind.
    He saw it coming so clear and defined!

And I never knew him.

A human failing? The need to survive?
We may be living, but are we alive?
With empty phrases and shallow prayers
his people deny him; the blame is theirs.

"I never new him".

Martin John Nicholls

99 Easter Garden
(John 20:16)

Minutes earlier she had been crying,
Anguished that her Lord had vanished,
No peace even in death.
Recognition came in a word, her name, spoken by Him,
Yes, He was alive!, Christ has Risen!

Reason for living returned to Magdalene,
Again she could see the beauty of the morning,
Begin to live once more, as she had since meeting Jesus.
Bright the eyes, mirroring the saved soul,
Only Christ could bring about that change.
Now hear the messenger "Christ is Risen"
"I have gone before you into a Galilee that is world wide.

Y Mochyn Daear

100

There in a garden, when God called my name
I could not face him because of my shame.
Trust I had broken, I ate from his tree
God forgive Adam, for Adam is me.

There in a garden Christ knelt down in prayer,
I helped them find him and I led them there.
They took and killed him on Calvary's tree.
God forgive Judas, for Judas is me.

There in a courtyard, as Jesus was tried
I do not know him - three times I replied
There as a cock crowed was my treachery.
God forgive Peter, for Peter is me.

There in a garden he rose from his tomb,
When we were hiding he entered the room.
Doubt not my living, my wounds you can see.
God forgive Thomas, for Thomas is me.

Now in my life Lord, in my every day
I need your guidance to show me my way.
Faithless and fearful no more let me be
Be my forgiveness and come alive in me.

Colin Ferguson

101　Easter Litany of Hope in Anger

In the beginning was the Word.. echoing in the chaos
The thread in the fabric of creation.

When God spoke, the word was Love
　　love on the earth
　　love in the skies
　　love on the streets
　　love in the churches
　　love in the houses
　　love in people's minds.. love in all places.

But love was hijacked
　　love was used
　　love was tortured
　　love was violated
　　love was crucified
　　love died.. and then the word was silenced.

Yet God spoke again
　　and this word was "but"
　　this word was "struggle"
So the Spirit danced in a rage
and Christ danced on his grave.

The evening star says to the night "I disagree"

Because Good Friday is replaced by Easter
Because Tomorrow follows Yesterday
Because the Son rises in the morning
Because there is Redemption.

We pledge ourselves to God in loving anger

Ludy Roper

102 We are astonished, Father,
that you have chosen us,
such ordinary people.
If we have any talent at all,
it is far outweighed by what we lack.

Yet in your wisdom and grace
you have given us the task
of sowing the seed.

Forgive us
that we noticed the weeds more than the corn.
We are sorry
that we are anxious about our failure.

Teach us to trust your wisdom,
for in grace you have brought everyone here today
and if we play our part
your Spirit will attend to the harvest
with its first fruits:
Jesus your Son

Tony Burnham

103

Concerning the why and how and what and who
of ministry,
one image keeps surfacing:

a table that is round.

It will take some sawing
to be roundtabled,
some redefining
and redesigning.
Such redoing and rebirthing
of narrowlong churching
can painful be
for people and tables.

It would mean no daising and throning,
for but one King is there,
and he was a footwasher, at table no less.
We must be loved into roundness,
for God has called a People,
not "them and us"

At one time

our narrowlong churches
were built to resemble the cross
but it does no good for buildings to do so
if lives do not.

Roundtabling means
no preferred seating,
no first and last,
no better and no corners
for "the least of these".

Roundtabling means
room for the Spirit
and gifts
and disturbing profound peace for all-

We can no longer prepare for the past.

We are called
to be Church,
and if he calls for other than roundtable,
we are bound to follow -

leaving the sawdust and chips,
designs and redesigns
behind,
in search of the Kingdom
(often hidden, always present)
which is his
and not ours.

Chuck Lathrop

104 Methuselah looks back

I've never been a member of FURY -
and this is sad to relate,
for when FURY was formed it happened
to be past my "sell by" date.
We grew up with Young People's Fellowships,
and socials with churches nearby.
There was an annual meeting at Swanwick,
but for places I never did try.
Down the years I've noted the changes,
and from afar I've looked on the scene
as younger faces have come to the forefront,
and filled the years between.
With fellowship of wider choice
forging overseas links as well,
Giving voice in debate at all levels
A Christian experience to tell.
Yardley Hastings and Ginger Groups offering
in many churches a part to play
with friendship and music and witness.
So speaks our Gospel through FURY today.

Anon

105   Oh give me your pity, I'm on a committee
Which means that both morning and night
We attend and amend and contend and defend
Without a conclusion in sight.
We confer and concur, we defer and demur
And re-iterate all of our thoughts.
We revise the agenda with frequest addenda,
And consider a load of reports.
We compose and propose, we support and oppose,
And the points of procedure are fun!
But though various notions are brought up as motions,
There's terribly little gets done,
We resolve and absolve, but NEVER dissolve,
Since that's out of the question for us.
What a shattering pity to end our Committee
Where else could we make such a fuss?

Anon

106   The Twelve Months of Yardley

In the first month of the centre the chaplain showed to me
a National Youth Secretary.

In the second month of the centre the Chaplain showed to me
two FURY Councils and a National Youth Secretary.

In the third month of the centre the Chaplain showed to me
three NYCs*, two FURY Councils and a National Youth Secretary.

In the fourth month of the centre the Chaplain showed to me
four sets of minutes, three NYCs, two FURY Councils
and a National Youth Secretary.

In the fifth month of the centre the Chaplain showed to me
five FURY words, four sets of minutes, three NYCs,
two FURY Councils and a National Youth Secretary.

In the sixth month of the centre the Chaplain showed to me
six CTMs**, five FURY words, four sets of minutes, three NYCs,
two FURY Councils and a National Youth Secretary.

In the seventh month of the centre the Chaplain showed to me
seven Pick 'n Mixes, six CTMs, five FURY words,
four sets of minutes, three NYCs, two FURY Councils
and a National Youth Secretary.

In the eighth month of the centre the Chaplain showed to me
eight working parties, seven Pick 'n Mixes, six CTMs,
five FURY words, four sets of minutes, three NYCs,
two FURY Councils and a National Youth Secretary.

In the ninth month of the centre the Chaplain showed to me
nine Trainers talking, eight working parties,
seven Pick 'n Mixes, six CTMs, five FURY words,
four sets of minutes, three NYCs, two FURY Councils
and a National Youth Secretary.

In the tenth month of the centre the Chaplain showed to me
ten Walks of Life, nine Trainers talking, eight working parties,
seven Pick 'n Mixes, six CTMs, five FURY words,
four sets of minutes, three NYCs, two FURY Councils
and a National Youth Secretary.

In the eleventh month of the centre the Chaplain showed to me
eleven Elders sleeping, ten Walks of Life,
nine Trainers talking, eight working parties, seven Pick 'n Mixes,
six CTMs, five FURY words, four sets of minutes, three NYCs,
two FURY Councils and a National Youth Secretary.

In the twelfth month of the centre the Chaplain showed to me,
twelve Provincial synods, eleven Elders Sleeping,
ten Walks of Life, nine Trainers talking, eight working parties,
seven Pick 'n Mixes, six CTMs, five FURY words,
four sets of minutes, three NYCs, two FURY Councils
and a National Youth Secretary.

Members of Fury Council

*   National Youth Committees,
**   Community Team Members

107   The rain falls on the just and unjust

We normally pick a good week,
Hot, sunny and dry.
We go out to the beach
Swimming, walking, water fights,
Football, rounders.

When we get a bad week
There are two sides to the coin.

Boys enjoy their week,
A sense of fellowship, of being together.
Staying up late, getting wet, muddy.
Keep on going when they've been up all night.
Of reveille at 7 am. At the beginning they
get up early, at the end they stay in bed.

Of Officers being on guard 24 hours a day
Is the canvas going to break, will the marquee
fall down, are the ground sheets holding out?
Preparing drink and food when it is cold,
keeping people motivated, organising games.
Of not being let off to go to the pub
because your concern is for the boys and the site.

And when we get home we say to our friends
The weather was terrible
and we were up all hours of the day.
The boys go home and say
We've had a brilliant time,
The best camp we've had.

A B Royal

108 White Horses

A dozen hearts are seized,
as darkness is falling.
A voice, it is calling
to ride on the swell.
It's blowing' East nor' East,
and gustin' six or seven,
for many this is heaven,
but for someone this is hell.

    Ride, boys, ride!
    Ride the white horses,
    silver-white horses,
    the race has begun.
    Time and tide are running against you,
    there's life to be rescued
    and a race to be won!

"When horses are so wild,
they never can be broken".
No truer word was spoken
of ocean or sea.
Many may have tried
to claim them and name them,
we'll never ever tame them,
they must have their liberty.

    Ride, boys, ride.....

    you know the stakes are high
    as you sail into the eye
    of the wind that cuts like a knife,
    but you make your sacrifice,
    who can put a price
    on a human life?

The sea is their domanin
and history shows sadly
they will not suffer gladly
the madness of fools.
They're pleasure and they're pain,
these beasts have their beauty;
our God-given duty
is to play by their rules.

    Ride, boys, ride....

Martin John Nicholls
Dedicated to the crew of Swanage Lifeboat

109 I felt a stranger

Arriving in Guyana, having reached this place at last,
I was a stranger in these unknown parts
With mysteries of earth and skies and now an intruder
In this forest world.

Striding into the lush, green foliage,
Twisting and turning a hundred-fold
Standing still and silent to peer
At the technicolour butterfly.

Sensitive to melodies and rhythms
Reaching into my body and mind
Exploring the glistening undergrowth
With expectations of unknown life.

The more I walked, the more I looked
The more I touched, the more I smelt
The less a stranger did I feel
In this exciting wilderness.
I was at one with the creator
Knowing a much deeper love,
Sharing with the other person
Rich experience of this time and place.

Sandra Ackroyd

110   You could call it the wedding of the year
to see her going down the aisle,
So happy, she was saying hello as she went
And the singing was simply tremendous
with the beating of the drum.

But now it's all over.
I see her from time to time.
Two brothers left but not the same
They have each other but something is gone
A sister who was always there.

Wendy Manners

111   Breaking Free

The pressure of society grows stronger day by day
People looking down on you for what you do and say,
Comments whispered snidely, eyes pressed upon your back,
Talents lost in favour of all those things you lack.
There are people teasing others for being fat or far too thin
And some ignored as penance for the colour of their skin.
And as I stand surrounded by all that's going on,
I watch the hurt inflicted and I know it's all so wrong,
For all that really matters is what's developing inside,
Our bodies are a dwelling place for the part of us we hide.
I know that God is watching and He simply doesn't care
About whether we are "popular" or how we do our hair.
And I'm so glad that He loves me,
that He sees through the pretence,
That hurtful words have made me form to act as my defence.
For I'm scared of feeling all alone,
I' m scared to expose "me"
In case I'm not considered the kind of person I should be,
According to unwritten rules that stand like solid steel,
Dictating thoughts and actions and how I'm meant to feel.
But though it may be painful I will try to drop those chains,
There may be many losses but I know there'll be more gains,
For God has gently told me that I' m loved for evermore,
And that He'll stand beside me through all that lies in store,
So my ears can bear the comments and my back can brave the stares.
For if everyone deserts me, I'll still know that Jesus cares.

Claire Seal

112   Dreams and Visions
(Joel 2.2)

I live in a world
Where everyone smiles.
There is no need
To cry,
To frown,
To feel sad.
There is
No hunger,
No thirst,
No war.

I live in a world
Where Your Word is Gospel.
There are feelings
Of faith,
Of hope,
Of love-
There is
No prejudice,
No hate,
No lies.

I live in a world
Where old people dream dreams
And young people see visions.
Can you visualise my dream world?

Melanie Smith

113   A Dream

Last night I had a dream
A dream where I saw Britannia
on bended knee;
Her tear filled eyes I could
clearly see,
Tears for a world that somehow
had forgotten how to care,
For the victims of violence -
for those that are homeless -
unemployed and knowing despair.

I saw in her eyes her concern
for the young -
her tears for the old,
Her worries for the future and
what it may hold.
Last night I dreamed I saw
Britannia on bended knee,
With arms outstretched, her head
bowed low -
to the soul of the nation she
made a plea,
For those blinded from the truth -
so that they might see,
That mankind could come together
to live in peace and harmony.

Then I awoke - the images still
hauntingly sharp,
And I thought of the things that
are tearing at our nation's heart;
And so I began to pray,
That with God's help we could find
a better way,
To a world where men and women can
walk tall and free,
Where mankind walks a straighter path -
for a better place this world to be;
A world where it doesn't matter about
creed or kin,
Where everyone cares for his fellow man
regardless of their origin,
And with God's help we could all win,
And there's a sign on everybody's door
that says....
Welcome in.

Peter Morriss

114   Are you coloured?
I am black, I always will be black.
When I am hot I am black,
When I am cold I am black,
When I was born I was black,
When I die I will be black.

You are white, you are never the same,
When you are hot you are red,
When you are cold you are blue,
When you are born you are pink,
When you die you are grey.
And you have the cheek to call me coloured.

Rebecca Coles

115 Alone

I' m alone, yet I'm with you
Nothing yet told
Open up let me reach you
Let's begin to unfold
I have left home and family
Friends who would feel I have nothing to offer
But a love that is real
So weak I am meeting you
But God is strong
Let us trust in each other
Come together as one.

Mary Hamilton

116 Hard Times

For the money to buy the clothes
Or to pay the landlord's rent
For the money to allay my woes
I just can't find the first cent.
Some blame it on their neighbours,
Others blame it on a friend
And those who have no one to blame, but themselves
Blame the Government

Euthman Wray

117

What do I see on these walls?
Whitewashed, Graffiteed, made home.
Do I see my pretty pictures?
Do I see photo's of home?

I think not really, however,
Of gloomy thoughts of doom.
I think of a chance to witness
Of your glorious love made new.

Elizabeth Watkins-Smith

118   The giro comes today

I took my son into school to his classroom. He was greeted by a classmate. As I knew him already I said "Hello" and asked him how things were going. He said, "The giro comes today". "Good", I said. "We'll get money to buy things", he continued. I rummaged around in my pockets for the packet of crisps we had bought on our way to school for breaktime consumption. "You're lucky" the boy said to my son, "you've got crisps!" I looked at the boy with more care, and noticed that his clothing was well worn and bore transfers of a TV super hero who was in vogue at least four years ago. He was pale and thin. I asked him, "Didn't you have any breakfast?" "No", he said. "So when did you last eat?" "We had some bread and "marge" yesterday for tea." I knew his family. Mum and dad went everywhere with the children and they attended everything that was to do with their children. Both parents were unemployed, but watching them say good-bye to their kids in the morning at school you could see the love and affection there. This was not a child of a profligate home, but a home of love and care. They had come to the end of the fortnight's giro and they had nothing left to eat. They had no money. I was overwhelmed by anger and sadness. In all likelihood if there was only enough for bread and margarine for the children, the parents were doing without for at least a couple of days. This is a nation whose leader is on record as saying he wants to create, "A nation at ease with itself". I gave the boy enough money to buy crisps at breaktime from the tuck-shop and left with tears of anger and impotent rage in my eyes.

From The Next Rung Down, N W Province

119   Too close to home

It was story time, the end of the day. I sat the children down for the story before they went home. I had chosen Hansel and Gretel. I began in the usual way, describing the woodcutter and the wicked stepmother who decided to get rid of the two children as there wasn't enough food for them all. Then I noticed two of my children were crying. The story was really disturbing them. It was a little while later that I realised the story was probably too close to their own home situation. Some of us teachers used to bring food in, cereals and the like, to give the kids we knew to be in homes with little money available to buy something to eat. The teachers knew they rarely had a breakfast. How can you expect a child to learn with an empty stomach?

From The Next Rung Down, N W Province

120

This is a poem about destroying,
Being unkind and annoying.
So much is dying everywhere.
People on earth they don't care.
Folks going out into combat.
Putting on uniform and a hard hat.
Not caring if the bullets fly,
People get wounded or they die.
Red, green, khaki and brown.
All these colours make me frown.
Red is the blood, the rest uniform.
Some people's babies aren't ever born!
We've got to call "stop" before it's too late,
We'll destroy the whole world at this rate.

This is a poem about recreation.
Renewing things all over the nation.
When things are growing everywhere.
And people's hearts show they care.
A time to make and to build
And see the earth has been tilled.
Then all the seeds are sown.
Sometime later they have grown,
making food for us to eat.
Let's share it with those we meet.
Also with people far and near.
Make their hunger disappear.
Can we start all over again;
Banish starvation and the pain?

Nicholas Clark

121 Yugoslavia

The guns blast out
And the children scream.
They look for an end,
If they dare to dream.
Lost and alone,
Abused and afraid,
All innocence gone in this mad charade.

The women cry
As the pain goes on,
And the child will be born
Before too long.
Bruised and in pain,
All dignity lost
As the struggle for power will not count the cost.

The men would cry,
If they thought it right,
But they hear the demand,
So they go to fight.
For women and children
Their struggle goes on,
But the life of the people they fight for is gone.

And God will scream,
And God will cry,
And God will demand
Us to answer "why?"
And God is bruised,
And God is in pain,
As God watches us crucify Christ again.

Anne J Sardeson

Index of first lines

Index of authors

Index of titles